# Getting More Out of Confession

## SOMETHING MORE FAITH SERIES

By Joel Stepanek

Mark Hart, Series Editor

Published by The Word Among Us Press
7115 Guilford Drive, Suite 100
Frederick, Maryland 21704

22 21 20 19 18    1 2 3 4 5

ISBN: 978-1-59325-339-4

Nihil Obstat:   Msgr. Michael Morgan, J.D., J.C.L.
                Censor Librorum
                April 3, 2018

Imprimatur:     +Most Rev. Felipe J. Estévez, S.T.D.
                Diocese of St. Augustine
                April 3, 2018

Cover design by Suzanne Earl
Cover photo by Dennis Crews

Made and printed in the United States of America

# Contents

Introduction: A New Beginning / 4

How to Use This Booklet / 6

Session 1: The Waiting Room / 8

Session 2: Broken Windows / 14

Session 3: What's Normal? / 22

Session 4: The Mess / 28

Session 5: Positive Growth / 34

# A New Beginning

By Mark Hart
Something More Series Editor

As a child, did you ever say "Sorry" to a brother or sister because your mom or dad made you do it? Maybe you hit someone or refused to share with another child, and you got caught. In an effort to teach you right from wrong, a parent forced you to look your sibling or friend in the eyes and apologize for the action. Maybe you apologized out of fear of further punishment but without any true sorrow for your actions.

Some people say they are sorry to God—and to others—strictly because they fear the consequences. We might regret the action due to the punishment it brings but not in and of itself. As we grow closer to God, however, we begin to see that sin is less about breaking rules and more about breaking the Father's heart.

That's because sin hurts or destroys relationships—with God and others. As Joel Stepanek points out in this booklet, we can restore that relationship—and he shows us step-by-step how that happens in the Sacrament of Reconciliation.

## Meet the Divine Physician

Joel also reminds us that Jesus is the Divine Physician. Jesus respects our free will, so he won't force us to come to him for forgiveness and mercy. But he is always waiting for us to come to him. He wants to heal us and make us whole again.

In the pages that follow, you are going to be reintroduced to one of the greatest blessings of our Catholic faith: the Sacrament of Reconciliation. Joel's passion for Confession truly reflects the man of God he is striving to be: imperfect but self-aware, with a deep and fervent love for God and his family. As he shares anecdotes from his own life and the Biblical roots of this sacrament, you'll grow to appreciate it as well.

## Encounter Jesus in the Sacrament

Perhaps you already love Confession, or possibly it's your least favorite thing to do. Whatever the case, if you want to become all that God intended you to be, this sacrament is critical to your life. My hope is that after these five sessions, you are able to acknowledge where you have fallen short and humbly seek to do something about it by making Confession a regular part of your life. As Joel reminds us, God takes what is broken in us and makes it new again. So what are we waiting for?

I pray this booklet will fire you up with a passion for the sacrament, as it did for me. The feeling I now experience approaching the confessional is nothing less than utter joy. Why? Because I know I will encounter Jesus and his healing love and mercy. May you, too, will have the same experience each time you come to the Divine Physician.

# How to Use This Booklet

Whether used individually or in a small group, each session of *Getting More Out of Confession* is designed to take under an hour. If you use it on your own, remember to begin and end each session with prayer. You might also want to find someone to talk to about what you're learning.

If you are part of a small group, the following guidelines can help you have a fruitful experience.

1. Establish a prayerful environment by taking time to pray before beginning. Ask the Holy Spirit to be with your group. Pray, "Come, Holy Spirit" slowly several times. Allow for a few moments of silence. Then say a prayer together, like the Our Father or Hail Mary or Glory Be.

2. Have one or two people read the Scripture passage aloud that appears at the beginning of each session.

3. Encourage everyone to read the commentary beforehand. You might ask one or two people to summarize the main points or say what most struck them from the reading.

4. Discuss the questions, being careful not to rush to the next one, especially if not everyone has spoken. Some people need more time to gather their thoughts. Some may need a moment of silence before they feel free to express themselves.

5. If the discussion strays, try to bring it back to the questions or the text. Any member of the group should feel free to gently steer the discussion to the next point.

6. When you are finished with the questions, the group facilitator should outline the "Challenge" section at the end and ask whether anyone has any questions about it. Encourage participants to do the suggested challenge.

7. End with prayer. Perhaps someone could pray spontaneously, thanking God for the opportunity to gather together to pray and study God's word.

8. Make sure you know when and where you are gathering for the next session. Participants will get the most out of each small group session if they read the Scripture passage and commentary and reflect on the questions before the group gathers again.

## GET THE MOST OUT OF YOUR BOOKLET

Before each session, visit **wau.org/faithseries** for a short video from the author.

# The Waiting Room

**Mark 2:17**

> "Those who are well have no need of a physician, but those who are sick; I came not to call the righteous, but sinners."

The emergency waiting room is the last place a parent wants to be on a Saturday afternoon. But there I was with my eighteen-month-old daughter, who had fallen and cut the bridge of her nose. Amid the noise and flutter of activity, I looked around at all the other people and remembered the times I had wound up there. Though people come to the ER for different reasons, we all have the same purpose: we are there to be healed.

Several weeks later, on a Saturday afternoon, I found myself waiting again, but this time it was in a line for Confession. Nobody was rushing around—in fact, only a few people sat quietly around me. Each of us got up, in the order in which we had arrived, to enter the "treatment room." And while all of us were there for different reasons, we all had the same purpose: we were there to be healed.

Healing is the goal in both scenarios, but for most of us, the emergency room seems far more about life and death than does the confessional. Far fewer people are rushing to seek Confession when they have a serious spiritual injury. We are more likely to try to justify the problem or fix it ourselves.

But there are some injuries we can't fix. When I've been to the emergency room—whether it was to get my chin stitched, a broken bone evaluated, or a concussion dealt with—it was for something that I could not heal myself. Before taking my daughter to the emergency room, I recognized that the wound she had sustained was beyond my ability to fix.

But I knew where I could bring her. I knew where the doctor was. It would have been foolish for me to pretend as if what had happened to her was "not a big deal." She had to have stitches (six of them, to be exact). That was what was necessary for her wound to heal.

I don't always treat spiritual injury the same way I treated my daughter's injury. I pretend as if my spiritual wounds aren't that bad and I can fix them on my own. I think many of us do this. Even if we think there is a problem, we often try to use some other remedy or cure.

Many people have tried to heal spiritual brokenness using exercise, diet, distraction, hobbies, or self-help books. None of those are bad things, and some of them are necessary in healing the effects of spiritual brokenness. But none can heal the root cause. Confession fixes the wound.

People often look at the confessional with a sense of confusion or even fear. These kinds of questions may arise:

*What really is a sin, anyway?*
*Are my sins really enough to hurt me? Doesn't God just automatically forgive everyone?*
*Why do I need to confess my sins to anyone, let alone a priest?*

To many people, even those who were raised Catholic, the Sacrament of Reconciliation seems archaic and unnecessary. It can seem cruel to make someone explain to another person the ways in which they've failed, all while sitting or kneeling in a small room.

> **Jesus offers us his mercy, healing, and redemption, and then he waits for our response.**

But what if Confession has something more to offer us? What if this sacrament is less about punishment and more about encounter—and an encounter not with judgment but with love and mercy itself?

## The Divine Physician

Jesus has many titles attributed to him by others and a few that he attributed to himself. One of the titles Jesus gave himself is that of Divine Physician. He didn't use those exact words, but he explained the role perfectly:

> And the scribes of the Pharisees, when they saw that he was eating with sinners and tax collectors, said to his disciples, "Why does he eat with tax collectors and sinners?" And when Jesus heard it, he said to them, "Those who are well have no need of a physician, but those who are sick; I came not to call the righteous, but sinners." (Mark 2:16-17)

Jesus said something that put everyone on edge: he came for people who are sick. That is all of us, but a few people listening to Jesus didn't get it. They didn't think they needed healing; they thought they were already righteous. So they made up excuses and walked away from his mercy.

Jesus came to heal the wounds that sin has caused. He

doesn't pick and choose whom to treat; he fixes up anyone who arrives. We just have to show up.

God is love (1 John 4:8). Love doesn't put pressure on us, and Jesus won't heal someone who refuses to seek healing. That isn't because he is cruel but because he respects our freedom. If suddenly Jesus began healing us when we didn't ask for it, it would be a gross violation of our free will. So Jesus offers us his mercy, healing, and redemption, and then he waits for our response.

Jesus' waiting doesn't mean he is passive. Jesus seeks us out, to invite us to receive his mercy and healing. He invites us into mercy, because that is his disposition and attitude—his very nature. Scripture confirms this, and throughout this booklet, we will recount several narratives where Jesus demonstrates his mercy in a powerful way. We will witness the great love and care of the Divine Physician.

Christ's powerful love can heal the broken places in our lives. In the Sacrament of Reconciliation, we regularly encounter Jesus, an encounter that will transform us. We all need the Divine Physician.

The doctor is in. It's time to see him.

## Questions for Reflection and Discussion

1. In what ways does a trip to the emergency room compare with going to Confession? How does this comparison change the way you view this sacrament?

2. Read Mark 2:13-17, the passage from which the verses about the Divine Physician are taken. Imagine yourself as a scribe and then as Levi, the tax collector. With whom do you most identify? Why?

3. If you see Confession as a punishment, why is that the case? Have you ever experienced Confession as an encounter? What was that like?

4. Why does Jesus wait for us to come to him for healing? What might prevent you from approaching him?

5. If you go to Confession infrequently or not at all, why are you seeking to learn more about Confession? What do you hope to get out of these sessions?

Lord, help me be open to what you want to offer me through these sessions on the Sacrament of Reconciliation. Allow me to accept your love in a new way. I want to recognize the places where I am broken. Help me trust in your powerful mercy.

If you were planning to read this book alone, consider giving a copy to your spouse or a friend and reading it with them. Use the questions for reflection as a starting point for a discussion.

If you are reading this as part of a faith group, ask a neighbor, coworker, or family member to be part of that group.

**Psalm 51:1-2**

Have mercy on me, O God,
according to your merciful love;
according to your abundant mercy blot out
my transgressions.
Wash me thoroughly from my iniquity,
and cleanse me from my sin!

For many years, I was a youth minister at a parish. One vivid memory that stands out from those years is the night a teenager broke a window at a retreat center. It was a very large plate-glass window. He was playing pool with some guys and attempted a trick shot, which sent the cue ball flying at high speed through the giant window.

The retreat center was in Wisconsin. It was the middle of January.

I'll never forget how sheepishly this high school senior approached me. The typically proud stature of this three-sport varsity athlete had diminished to a slump. I knew something had happened. "Joel," he said, "I broke a window."

Maybe you've had a similar experience. Breaking a window, or breaking anything, is something you can't run from. People may not always know if you are lying or being dishonest, but if you crash a friend's car, they are going to find out.

Sin, too, breaks something. It causes real damage, both eternally and in the "right now." In order to make things right, we need to go through a process.

We call Confession the Sacrament of Reconciliation for a reason. Reconciliation is a process, and we go through it to restore relationships. If we do something that hurts or breaks a relationship, the only way to really restore it is through the process of reconciliation.

There are five movements to the process of reconciliation. To get more concrete, let's think about that teen whose dream of becoming a trick-shot pool player turned into a lot of shattered glass and a drafty retreat center. While his window-breaking was not intentional and therefore not a sin, it still required reconciliation.

1. A wrong is committed. (A window was broken.)
2. We feel bad about the thing we did. (The window breaker felt guilty.)
3. An apology is offered to the person we hurt. (He told me what happened and apologized.)
4. The person we hurt forgives us. (I forgave him.)
5. We make restitution for any harm done. (We paid for the window.)

## Smashing Pumpkins

One night my friends and I went out smashing pumpkins. I knew it was a horrible thing to do, and I felt especially terrible about one house where I destroyed a giant pumpkin. All night I stayed awake thinking about it. The next day, I went to that house to pay for the pumpkin.

The family was outside cleaning everything up. I went up to the mother and asked about the destroyed squash.

One of the kids chimed in, "We had a huge pumpkin that someone smashed all over the road." My heart sank. When the moment came for me to admit that I was the one who did it, I was too scared. I told the mother that my friends had done it and that I felt bad and wanted to pay on their behalf. I made restitution for the harm I did, but I never reconciled with that family.

> We don't want to risk becoming complacent and comfortable with our sins or justify them and make excuses for them.

I still think about that pumpkin.

When we make restitution for our wrongs, we sometimes think that we have made things "right" and can bypass the whole reconciliation process. We might buy a gift for someone we have hurt but never apologize. Thus, we hope to "make it up to them." But the relationship never really heals, because we aren't reconciled.

Some people believe that they "just need to tell God" or that "God already knows what I've done; I just need to make it right." That was my argument for why I didn't tell the family that I had smashed their pumpkin. What can apologizing really do, my thought was, other than make the situation more awkward? Well, a lot, actually.

If we want the healing that comes from being reconciled with God, we need to follow the process that happens in the Sacrament of Reconciliation. This is why Jesus gives us the sacrament: it walks us through the five steps and allows us to really be reconciled with God.

We can't do this on our own. Jesus gives priests and bishops special authority to act on his behalf to forgive our sins and reconcile us to him and the Church. We say that they act *in persona Christi capitis*, a Latin phrase that translates as "in the person of Christ, the head." Jesus is the head of the body of Christ, the Church (Colossians 1:18), and the only one with the authority to forgive sins (Mark 2:10).

With a priest acting *in persona Christi capitis*, we walk through the Sacrament of Reconciliation the same way that we reconcile with another person in our lives:

1. We commit a sin.

Probably a few of them—some minor and some major.

2. We feel bad about our sins and seek forgiveness.

When we walk into the confessional, we say, "Bless me, Father, for I have sinned." We admit that we have fallen short. We share how long it has been since we last received the sacrament and then list our sins.

This is important. We need to name our sins explicitly, because this allows us to take ownership of our actions. We don't want to risk becoming complacent and comfortable with our sins or justify them and make excuses for them. Instead of blaming someone else, we blame ourselves and acknowledge that we fell short in specific ways.

Naming our sins is the opposite of what I did with the pumpkin. By naming our sins, we take away the power that silence and ignorance give to them.

3. We ask forgiveness.

After we name our sins, we ask forgiveness in a formal way. We call this "making an act of contrition." There are several such prayers you can memorize, or you can simply read one from a card. Oftentimes this prayer will be in the confessional, ready for you to read.

This isn't an empty ritual; in an act of contrition, we do three things. First, we express sorrow for our sins because they've hurt God and others. Second, we ask for forgiveness for our sins, confident that we are going to receive it. Finally, we make a commitment to avoid sin and to ask for God's grace and help in doing so.

4. Jesus forgives us.

The priest responds to our act of contrition with a prayer absolving us of our sins. Jesus has forgiven us through his death on the cross; he paid the price for our sin and took on the punishment for us. We don't need to pay for the broken window; he buys a new one for us.

This prayer is an affirmation that we are receiving the grace that poured forth from the cross. As the priest prays it, our sins are erased, and we are set free from their eternal consequences. Remember, this isn't the priest acting on his own power. It is Jesus Christ telling us that, through his death and resurrection, we are forgiven. This is a powerful moment, when we can be assured that we have been truly forgiven.

5. We make restitution.

We call this part of the Sacrament of Reconciliation *penance*. Our sin has an effect on the world around us, even if we don't see it. The penance the priest assigns us isn't a punishment; it's an opportunity to ask God to make things right. We offer up our penance for people we have hurt, we ask for even more grace to avoid sin, and we pray for the healing of any lingering effects of sin in our lives.

This isn't a part of the process to skip or forget. A great way to make sure you pray your penance is to offer it up right after Confession. If it's a penance you need to do more than once, set yourself a reminder to do it.

Reconciliation is a process that brings real healing and restoration to what is broken in our relationships with God and others, as well as what is broken within us. Jesus knows we need reconciliation, so he gave us a way to encounter him in a profound and real way through Confession.

Healing exists for the broken windows in our lives. Jesus not only pays the price, but he gives us new windows—he makes all things new.

## Questions for Reflection and Discussion

1. Think of a relationship in which you and the other person reconciled. In what ways did that bring healing and restoration? Was there something you could have done differently that would have speeded up the process or made it easier?

2. Are you sometimes tempted to bypass reconciling with someone you have hurt? What do you find difficult about asking for forgiveness?

3. Have you ever thought of Jesus not only forgiving you in the Sacrament of Reconciliation, but also restoring what was broken? How does that lead you to a better understanding of this sacrament?

4. How easy is it for you to forgive someone? What might cause you to hold on to resentment, even after you have accepted someone's apology?

5. How do you ordinarily think of penance? How does the description given in this session affect your view?

## Pray

Lord, help me to forgive others and to seek forgiveness. Help me especially to seek forgiveness from you. With your grace, allow reconciliation to be a part of how I live as a follower of Jesus Christ.

## Challenge

Jesus emphasizes our need to be reconciled with God but also to reconcile with each other. Read Matthew 5:22-26, and pray about whom you need to reconcile with. If possible, work toward reconciliation with that person.

> **Luke 19:5**
>
> And when Jesus came to the place, he looked up and said to him, "Zacchaeus, make haste and come down; for I must stay at your house today."

My kids are great at trying to rationalize their way out of wrongdoing. The other day, I caught my three-year-old son, Elijah, drawing on the wall with a crayon. When I asked him why he thought that was okay, he responded, "The paper is all filled up, and I was only going to draw in this little space!"

While Elijah's quick thinking is adorable, it's also maddening. When he comes up against a rule he doesn't like or does something that is going to get him in trouble, he always finds a way to explain away his action.

The truth is, we never really grow out of our ability to rationalize. We rationalize eating that last piece of cake: "Who else is going to eat that cake?" or "My diet starts tomorrow." We rationalize gossip: "I'm not hurting anyone, just passing along information." In fact, bad habits and sin are often rooted in rationalization.

It's always been that way. Adam and Eve were living in a perfect relationship with God and each other. They just needed to follow a simple rule: they couldn't eat the fruit from a particular tree. Because of God's gift of free will, this man and woman were able to make a choice. They could choose to trust God or choose to give in to a lie.

The serpent told Eve, "You will be like God, knowing good and evil" (Genesis 3:5). That's a pretty big temptation. Watch how the rationalization plays out:

> So when the woman saw that the tree was good for food, and that it was a delight to the eyes, and that the tree was to be desired to make one wise, she took of its fruit and ate; and she also gave some to her husband. (Genesis 3:6)

Did you catch that? Eve listened to the serpent and then said to herself, "You know, this tree doesn't look too bad. And being able to tell right from wrong? That doesn't seem like a bad thing either. Let's do this."

That is how quickly sin happens. It often starts with convincing ourselves that it's okay—even good—to do something wrong. Think about your own life—we've all done this. We think we can change the rules for that one moment. We even think those rules are holding us back rather than keeping us free.

But sin doesn't make us free. It makes us slaves. Sin always has consequences. Sin hurts, wounds, and can even destroy our relationships with God and with other people. We can try to rationalize it, but we can't escape the truth about sin.

## Zacchaeus the Tax Collector

One of my favorite stories in Scripture is about a short man named Zacchaeus (found in Luke 19:1-10). Zacchaeus was a tax collector. Tax collectors often became rich by taking much more than was necessary. They were seen as state-sponsored thieves.

I don't think I could take that much money from friends, family, and people in my community, but I'm sure the tax collectors rationalized it. They probably told themselves that this was just the way things were. Perhaps, deep down, they recognized the evil of their greed and how unjust it was. Maybe they had pangs of conscience when they took so much from a family that there wasn't enough left for the basics, like food. But they did it anyway. Sin numbs us to how much it hurts others (and ourselves).

> Likewise, when we are still stuck in our sins, even before we name them, Jesus is with us.

Zacchaeus was a tax collector, but he was also interested in Jesus. He climbed a tree just so he could see him. Then Jesus did something radical: he invited himself over for dinner.

People were shocked. Did Jesus not know who Zacchaeus was? Why was he going to eat a meal in a house that was built on money earned through sin? But Jesus is the Divine Physician. He was interested in healing Zacchaeus, not condemning him. He is the doctor who will refuse service to no one.

Zacchaeus was done with rationalizing his sin; he was done with being comfortable with the thing that hurt him most. He had a moment of conversion. He wasn't going to live the status quo anymore; he was going to live for Christ.

## It's Our Choice

It's easy for us to "normalize" sin and slip into sinful routines. Sometimes it's a minor bad habit that keeps us stuck.

Other times it's something major, like stealing or marital infidelity. We allow sin—both small and large—to exist in our lives because we normalize it.

Jesus wants to shake us up. After an encounter with him, we realize that we have a choice to make, just as Adam and Eve did: to trust him and turn our lives around or to choose against him and continue in slavery.

Calling out the places where you have normalized sin can be difficult. We get so used to sin, so numb to it, that it can take a while to root it out. Zacchaeus knew he needed to turn around. He told Jesus he would restore what he had taken and also give money to the poor.

But do you notice something? First Jesus encountered Zacchaeus, and then Zacchaeus named his sins and sought forgiveness and restitution. Likewise, when we are still stuck in our sins, even before we name them, Jesus is with us.

Habits form without our knowing in the hundreds of choices we make every day. Don't let sin be a part of that. Jesus is waiting for you to name your sins, so he can free you from them and call you to something more: true freedom.

Every choice that involves the opportunity to sin puts us in the same position as Adam and Eve were in. Do we choose our own path, believing it to be better than the freedom that God provides, or do we choose God's path? Do we take steps toward the normalcy of sin, or do we take steps toward virtue?

Zacchaeus encountered Christ and rejected a way of life that had become normal for him. It's our turn to take the same step. Let's recognize sin for what it is: a mess of brokenness.

The good news is that Jesus doesn't abandon us in our mess. Instead, he enters into it.

1. How did Adam and Eve rationalize their disobedience? How does Genesis 3:6 help you understand ways that you rationalize sin in your life?

2. Read the story of Zacchaeus in Luke 19:1-10. What was it about Zacchaeus' encounter with Jesus that caused him to turn from his former lifestyle so quickly?

3. Do you believe that Jesus wants you to draw near to him even in your sin? How might you encounter Jesus in the same way Zacchaeus did?

4. When has sin taken hold in your life without your realizing it? How did you break the cycle of sin?

5. Where has sin become "normal" in our culture? How does this affect our ability to avoid sin and pursue holiness?

## Pray

Lord Jesus Christ, help me become aware of the places in my life where I fall short. I know that if I bring those areas to you, you will not condemn me but will heal me with your merciful love. Give me the gift of sorrow for my sins.

I believe that, with your grace, my choices in the face of temptation can be for you and the love and freedom you offer.

## Challenge

A first step in rooting out sin is identifying where it has a foothold in your life. Think about the many choices you face each day. Which ones can lead you to trust God? Which ones could lead you to give in to sin?

A great way to do this is to write out your schedule. At what times and in what situations does sin creep in?

# SESSION FOUR

## The Mess

**Revelation 21:5**

"Behold, I make all things new."

Regret is an awful feeling. Sometimes it creeps in slowly after the fact, and sometimes it is immediate. The first time it happened for me, I felt it right away. I was five years old.

I had a special coloring book. The fun part of the book was that I had to draw half of the picture freehand. I could create something beautiful in imitation of the example on the other half of the page.

I loved that book. But I also hated my artwork. I looked at the perfection of the first half of each drawing, then at my part, and saw only the places where I didn't measure up. So one day, in a bout of frustration, I tore it all up. Not just one picture but the entire coloring book.

I will never forget the feeling as I sat in my room surrounded by torn pages. What had I done? In a single moment, I had torn my favorite coloring book to pieces. In the process, I tore myself apart as well.

When my mother found me, I was sobbing amid the pieces. I wanted my coloring book back. Even though I had been frustrated in that moment, there were still more pages to color—and opportunities to improve my drawing. But now they were all gone.

28

My mother said we would try to find another book like that one, but we never did. In a moment of anger, I had ruined the book, and I could never get it back.

As I got older, I often found myself sitting in a mess I had made through my sin. I would feel as if I had ruined everything. I would wish I could undo what I had done wrong.

We all know the feeling. Maybe it comes after sharp words find their way past our lips in a moment of anger. Or after exhaustion leads us to seek relief in dark places of the Internet, where we consume video after video. Or after stress pushes us way too far into that bottle.

At the end of it all, we have nothing to show but regret.

## Jesus Makes All Things New

Every time I found myself picking up the pieces of my life after sin, I wished I had remembered a verse at the end of the Bible, in the Book of Revelation. In a vision of Jesus' disciple, John, Jesus is sitting on a heavenly throne, and he says, "Behold, I make all things new" (Revelation 21:5).

Revelation speaks of a new heaven and a new earth, a place where there is no more suffering or sin, a place where we don't have to sit with pieces of a torn-up coloring book or the chains of destructive behaviors. Jesus makes all things new, and that includes you and me.

Sin has a cost. As much as we may try to convince ourselves that certain actions are "personal" and don't affect anyone else, we know that actions always have their consequences. For one thing, committing one sin often makes it easier to sin the next time.

In the Gospel of Matthew, Jesus is asked which commandment is the greatest. He responds with two:

> "You shall love the Lord your God with all your heart, and with all your soul, and with all your mind. This is the great and first commandment. And a second is like it, You shall love your neighbor as yourself." (Matthew 22:37-39)

Jesus' words underscore the priority he places on our relationships with God and our neighbor. Sin is any action that hurts, weakens, or even destroys those relationships.

**It is as if Jesus restores the pages of whatever we've torn up. He hands us something new. He makes *us* new.**

We can commit sins that only harm our relationship with God (like putting other things before God in our life). But we cannot sin against our neighbor without also sinning against God. Since God created all people in his image and likeness, anytime we hurt someone else, we also harm our relationship with God.

God could let things stay that way. He could find us sitting in our own mess and say to us, "You really bungled this, and it's your own fault. If you had made better choices, you wouldn't be in this mess."

But God doesn't let us sit in our mess. Instead God enters into it.

## Good News

The Nativity scene is good news. It shows us what life looks like when God enters into our world. God the Father sends God the Son, Jesus Christ, to be born into our mess and become like us in all things except sin (see Hebrews 4:15). Jesus comes to rescue us and help us become new. He comes to put back together what we've broken through sin.

To do this, however, Jesus takes on the consequences of our sin. Sin doesn't just have an effect in our own time; it also has an eternal effect. Since sin always harms our relationship with God, we need to do something to restore that relationship. In the case of the broken window, we offered to pay for a new one, and we did. If you break something, you may offer to pay for it or even repair it yourself.

But in our relationship with God, we can't do that. God is perfect and in need of nothing. We can't pay him back. So how do we fix our relationship with God after we've broken it through sin? There is no way we can do it.

That's why Jesus Christ was born into the world. As fully God and fully man, he bridges the gap between God and human beings that exists because of sin.

When I ripped up that coloring book, my mom sat down with me among the shredded paper and held me while I cried. She entered into my suffering. But my mom couldn't give me a new coloring book.

Jesus steps into our mess and enters into our suffering by taking on the only just punishment for our sins—death. This is where things are made new. Jesus dies on a cross, and then he is raised from the dead. It is in this dying and rising that sin is defeated.

It is as if Jesus restores the pages of whatever we've torn up. He hands us something new. He makes *us* new.

This is an incredible display of God's love and mercy. God the Father allows Jesus Christ, the Son, to take on the weight and punishment of our sins, so that our relationship with him can be restored. God doesn't abandon us to sin and death; instead he saves us. Jesus lays down his life freely for us. He offers us his healing mercy. We just have to decide if we want to accept it.

Regardless of what we've done or what we've torn up, mercy is waiting. We have the choice: Do we receive Jesus' mercy and forgiveness in Confession, or do we allow our pride to leave us sitting in our own mess?

There is beautiful freedom in accepting the forgiveness Jesus already won for us and in hearing the words of absolution. We encounter Christ, crucified and risen, speaking to us: "May God grant you pardon and peace. I absolve you of your sins." This is freedom. We all get a new coloring book and a chance to start over.

## Questions for Reflection and Discussion

1. How does the definition of sin as anything that hurts our relationship with God or neighbor differ from the way you have viewed sin? How does that description encompass all sin?

2. Think of a time when you felt as if you had seriously offended God, even though you may not have hurt anyone else. How did it affect your relationship with him?

3. Have you ever felt as if something you did destroyed everything? Were you able to find healing? If so, how? If not, what can you do now to pursue that healing?

4. Is there a mess in your life right now? What is it? Where do you need healing and restoration?

5. Through Jesus' death and resurrection, God makes all things new. Is this something you struggle to believe? Why or why not?

### Pray

Lord Jesus Christ, through your death and resurrection, you make all things new. I thank you for coming into the mess of this world to save me. Whatever I have done in the past, whatever I may do in the future, may I always come to you for forgiveness and healing.

### Challenge

Read through the narrative of Christ's crucifixion in any of the Gospels. As you read and meditate, thank God for the sacrifice he made for your freedom.

### Luke 7:41-43

"A certain creditor had two debtors; one owed five hundred denarii, and the other fifty. When they could not pay, he forgave them both. Now which of them will love him more?" Simon answered, "The one, I suppose, to whom he forgave more." And he said to him, "You have judged rightly."

*Good habitual practices produce positive growth.* This was my mantra as a personal trainer in college. I mentored and coached several clients every week, and I continually reminded them that their diligence and discipline would pay off in the long run.

Throughout this booklet, we've considered Jesus Christ, the Divine Physician, and the ways in which he encounters us through the various movements of the Sacrament of Reconciliation. Now it's time to have that encounter.

Maybe over the last few weeks you've been to Confession and experienced the healing mercy of Christ. Maybe you are preparing to go. Either way, it can't be a "one and done" experience. Despite our best efforts, we will continue to struggle with sin. We will continue to fall short of what God asks of us. If we want to approach a continually deeper relationship with Jesus—and eventually heaven—we need to make the Sacrament of Reconciliation a part of our regular routine.

Sometimes Confession is a profound experience; other times it may feel as if nothing has happened. But *good habitual practices lead to positive growth.* If we want to grow, we need to work at it—and that means doing things that are difficult. It isn't always convenient to get to Confession. Sometimes we are ashamed of what we have to confess. Sometimes we just don't feel like waiting in line.

But is reconciliation worth it? The answer is yes—it's always yes! The question we have to ask ourselves is this: How intent am I on making Confession a regular part of my relationship with Jesus?

## A Debt Forgiven

The woman has a reputation and is considered unclean, an outcast. But she has heard the stories about Jesus, about how he eats with sinners, heals the sick, and forgives sins. So she decides to let nothing stand in her way.

Jesus is eating dinner at the house of a Pharisee named Simon. The woman knows that the men there are likely to throw her out. She doesn't care. She goes there anyway and brings some expensive oil with her—probably purchased with money earned from her "trade."

She bursts through the door and falls at the feet of Jesus, already weeping. With her hair, she dries the tears that have wet his feet. Everyone is shocked—except Jesus. A woman who is "unclean" will make someone else unclean if she touches him. How is Jesus okay with this?

Simon is thinking, "If he was really a prophet, then he would know that this woman is a sinful person." Jesus knows Simon's heart, so he tells a parable. One person has a small debt forgiven, and one has a large debt forgiven. Which one will love the creditor more? Obviously, the one who has been forgiven more.

This woman breaks all social norms because she loves Jesus and knows he can heal her. She knows she needs the Divine Physician. The Pharisees need Jesus' love and mercy just as much as the woman does, but they refuse to recognize that. So in believing that they need little, they love little. The woman is intent on seeking forgiveness, and her reward is an increase in love (see Luke 7:36-50).

> Give God thanks and praise for the moments you avoided temptation, said or did the right thing, or overcame a sin.

For us, the question is, how much are we willing to love the one who forgives us? When we encounter the mercy of Christ—when we receive the healing of the Divine Physician—we cannot help but love him. In fact, the bigger our sin, the more we can realize we need Jesus and love him.

But if we don't recognize our need for a savior, then the process breaks down. We become self-righteous, ignorant of the large wound we carry around, and we love our Lord little.

## Examining Your Conscience

Two simple practices can help us become more like the woman who anoints Jesus' feet and less like the Pharisees. One we can do daily, and the other weekly or every few weeks. Both relate to how we encounter Jesus in the Sacrament of Reconciliation.

We can make a practice of examining our conscience. This simple reflection should always be done before we go to Confession, but it can be part of our daily prayer. We go back through our day and think about where we have fallen short, where we have sinned, where we have hurt our relationship with God and others, and where we need healing from our self-inflicted wounds.

Examining your conscience is not an exercise in guilt or feeling bad; it is looking for places where you can improve, places where you need God's mercy and grace, so you can grow closer to him. Athletes do a similar thing when they examine their performance: they discover where they aren't succeeding; then they work on those areas. If your goal is heaven, then you need to be aware of anything that might hinder you from achieving holiness.

It may be helpful to examine not only areas where you fell short but also places where God's grace is at work in you. Give God thanks and praise for the moments you avoided temptation, said or did the right thing, or over-came a sin. This helps you recognize and give thanks for God's faithfulness toward you.

There are several different ways you can make an examination of conscience. The easiest way is to reflect on the two great commandments: to love God with all your heart, soul, and mind and to love your neighbor as yourself (Matthew 22:37-39). Ask yourself, "Where did I live these two commandments well today? Where did I fail to live these two commandments?" Then take a few moments to either journal or reflect on where you succeeded with God's grace and where you failed.

It is important to note specific instances where you failed to love God and your neighbor. If we don't identify those areas where we need to grow, we will not grow at all.

Reflecting on the two great commandments is a good tool for daily reflection. Every few weeks, however, it is worthwhile going deeper by using a more detailed examination of conscience. There are many examinations online; some are longer than others and go into more specifics. Find one that helps you identify where you've fallen short and leads you to feel sorry for your sins.

Classic examinations of conscience revolving around the Ten Commandments are some of my favorites, and they are often presented as a series of questions. The United States Conference of Catholic Bishops has several great examinations online, at usccb.org. These include a general examination based on the Ten Commandments; separate examinations for young adults, married people, single adults, and children; and one based on Catholic social teaching. These longer examinations may not be a good fit for daily use but are worthwhile doing once a week and before going to Confession.

Remember, the goal isn't to make us feel awful for our sins but to help us feel sorry and push us toward receiving God's mercy. We need to name specific areas where we need healing. As we name them and take ownership of them, Jesus can forgive and heal us.

Jesus is the Divine Physician. He waits for us to recognize our need for a savior. We need to be bold and rush to him. He wants to heal us and make us new.

The next move is yours. Are you ready to be healed and made new?

1. In the parable about the sinful woman, Jesus links for-giveness with love. How can you grow in awareness of the great debt that God has forgiven you through Jesus? How might this increase your love of God?

2. What is the advantage of doing a daily examination of conscience? If you have done this in the past, how has it helped you? How might it help you going forward?

3. How can you integrate a daily examination of con-science into your routine? What time of day would work best for you?

4. What are some of the obstacles you encounter in getting to Confession regularly? How can you overcome these?

5. What or who can hold you accountable for receiving the Sacrament of Reconciliation frequently? Making an appointment on your calendar? Keeping track of when you last went to Confession? Asking your spouse or a friend to keep you accountable?

### Pray

Lord Jesus, I am ready to encounter you in Confession. Give me the courage to seek your mercy. Give me a clear mind to confess all my sins. Grant me the peace of knowing that your forgiveness is waiting for me. Provide me with the strength I need to go forward and "not sin again" (John 8:11).

### Challenge

Make a longer examination of conscience. Walk through the Ten Commandments, and ask where you've fallen short. Don't allow this to be a moment of shame. Use your contrition to move you to the Sacrament of Reconciliation this week.